The Mask We Wear

PAIN! HURT! FEAR!
UNFORGIVENESS!
These are all Spirits and they all have a
MASK!

Barbara A. Taylor

THE MASK WE WEAR

AUTHOR'S CONTACT INFO

Email:
Taylorjr54@gmail.com

Website:
www.barbaraataylor.com

Facebook:
https://www.facebook.com/Taylorjr5

Acknowledgements

God - the Father, Jesus - My Savior and The Holy Ghost - My Keeper.

My children, through the things I endured with them, helped me get to the place I am today. Thank you!

My church family who prayed for me - Thank you!

Thank you to - The late Superintendent, Bobby and Mrs. Rose Mae Price, Pastor Roger Jones II, Queen Bishop Marlyn S. and Dr. Freeman Thomas and the Life Line Family Worship Center church family, and others who had my back.

PAIN IS REAL

And so is God

CHAPTER ONE
Hurting

To all of you who are trying to MASK your pain - "Peek-A-Boo," God sees you. He wants to come to your rescue.

First, let's define the word – mask. Dictionary.com defines mask as a covering for all or part of the face, worn to conceal one's identity.

A mask is something we wear to cover our face, to hide from germs, or to keep people from seeing who we are. That is not the mask I am talking about. The mask I am referring to is when we hide behind smiles, laughter, goofiness, bullying, etc. to hide our pain.

As people of God, we hide behind hallelujah's, dancing and running around the church to mask hurt and pain. Often, we try to mask the pain of hurt, disappointment, fear, misuse, divorce, lost, shame, abuse, molestation, incest and many other things.

Most of my life, I have dealt with hurt and wore masks to

hide my feelings of being abandoned at the age of three. Don't let anyone tell you that a three-year old doesn't know what they are talking about or that they don't remember anything. I can tell you for a fact - they do. I wore the masks to hide my hurt and shame of not feeling good enough for my parents to love me and stay with me. I did not know that it was because of their selfishness that they left.

Mommy and Dad, I forgive you!

Growing up in a house where I felt I was the least of all, I encountered many hurts and pains. Living with my grandfather caused me to put on more masks. At the age of ten, I wanted to die because I felt so alone.

Watch your children!

When they begin staying to themselves, locked in a room and don't want to be with family - investigate that! Make sure they are not having bad thoughts; thoughts of suicide.

I never thought of killing myself because I read my bible and knew that was a No-No. However, I did want to die because of the way I was being mistreated.

At 16, I was beaten really bad by my grandfather. I looked like I had horns all over my body. He beat me because I asked him why he was talking about me and calling me all kind of names.

Grandfather, I forgive you!

I left my grandparent's house to go to my husband's house. An abusive husband! I stayed in that marriage for six years. I hid behind smiles, laughter, and shyness. I felt that if I opened my mouth, everything that I was going through would have spewed out like the exorcist.

Husband, I forgive you!

Pain is real and so are the masks we wear. We hide our hurt, disappointments, fear and pain behind masks so people won't be able to see the things we are going through or have gone through. I was ashamed and didn't want people to know that I was hurting or the depth of my despair. I didn't want anyone to know what I was going through, or how I was dealing with it.

My first marriage failed. Therefore, I put on another mask. A mask to hide the hurt, abuse and the shame I felt of not being able to hold my marriage together. I didn't realize that it took two people working together with God's help to make things work out.

Ex- Husband, I forgive you!

Scriptures to Read Concern Hurting

Psalms 27:13-14

I had fainted, unless I had believed to see the goodness of the Lord in the land of the living. Wait on the Lord: be of good courage, and he shall strengthen thine heart: wait, I say, on the Lord.

Philippians 4:6

Be careful for nothing; but in everything by prayer and supplication with thanksgiving let your requests be made known unto God.

Isaiah 41:10

Fear thou not; for I am with thee: be not dismayed; for I am thy God: I will uphold thee with the right hand of my righteousness.

I Peter 4:12-13

Beloved, think it not strange concerning the fiery trial which is to try you, as though some strange thing happened unto you: But rejoice, inasmuch as ye re partakers of Christ's sufferings; that, when his glory shall be revealed, ye may be glad also with exceeding joy.

St. Matthew 4:23-24

And Jesus went about all Galilee, teaching in their synagogues, and preaching the gospel of the kingdom, and healing all manner of sickness and all manner of disease among the people. And the fame went throughout all Syria: and they brought unto him all sick people that were taken with divers diseases and torments, and those which were possessed with devils, and those which were lunatic, and those that had the palsy; and he healed them.

Roman 8:28

And we know that all things work together for good to them that love God, to them who are the called according to his purpose.

Job 5:11
To set up on high those that be low; that those which mourn may be exalted to safety.

II Corinthians 1:3-4
Blessed be God, even the Father of our Lord Jesus Christ, the Father of mercies, and the God of all comfort; Who comforteth us in all our tribulation, that we may be able to comfort wherewith we ourselves are comforted of God.

Hebrew 13:4
Marriage is honorable in all, and the bed undefiled: but whoremongers and adulterers God will judge.

CHAPTER TWO
Fear, Doubt & Worry

I was afraid, doubtful and worried about whether I should have been married. I wrestled with the spirits of fear, doubt and worry.

Don't allow these spirits to invade your mind and body. You must pray, pray and pray again until you are free of them.

I stayed single for four years. One day I met this man who seemed like a good man. We began dating and he acted like he loved me. I felt that something was wrong, but I kept telling myself it was just me and my feelings.

Eventually, we broke up and during that time I gave myself to the Lord. I got saved. But you know once you get a touch of the goodie you keep wanting it, not realizing it was a trick of the enemy. Early in my new life, I backslid and started sleeping with him again.

I got pregnant!

We talked about getting married, and later that year we did.

Let me backup - when we started dating, I wanted to be

upfront about everything. I told him things about my past not knowing that it would come back to haunt me.

I was beginning to remove some of the masks, but before I could remove the mask of doubt, fear and worry, things began to go topsy-turvy as my granny used to say. That is when I began to hear – "I loved you but not enough to marry you," and "I want an annulment." That went on for a while and turned into "I want a divorce." I heard this for 19 years.

During those years, my husband would take me with him to his girlfriend's house. He would have me and the kids sit in the car while he did what he had to do. He would buy her clothes and sit them on our floor model TV so I could see them and wait for me to say something.

The worst kind of hurt one can experience is one that you cannot see and there is no medication to help heal it. This type of pain is like an infection. It begins to form a scab over the wound, but every time you get hurt again it bruises and gets infected again.

That pain lasted for years. I wore the masks of *I am fine* and well placed *hallelujahs*. One day I began to tell the Lord - Father, I have come to the end of my rope. I am going to tie a knot in it and try to hold on.

God gave me different words of encouragement. He said that He was working things out for me. He told me that He had not forgotten about me. God reminded me that my husband would reap what he sowed.

When God told me that, I stopped crying for myself and began to cry for my husband. I knew what I had gone through with him and because of him. I told the Lord he wouldn't be able to take it. I prayed, Father help him, he won't be able to take it. Why? Because he didn't have God in his life, it would be twice as rough as what he had put me through.

Now, this one - he didn't go to church, but he managed to start dating one of the women from my church. The bible does say those who take sweet counsel with you will kick up their heels against you. Was I upset with her? Yes, but I was more upset with him! God told me that the women in his life could only do what he allowed them to do.

I was still masking the hurt and pain. Yes, I knew that God can heal; He'd told me that years ago. But when you are in situations - the stress of the situation can feel like it's choking the life out of you.

Momentarily, you may forget the Word until you're able to catch your breath and think. But I still say -Yes; boldly, I say that God can heal you of any situation, circumstance or condition. He has not changed. There is a song by recording artist, Dottie Peoples, that says - *"what God did way back then He will do the same thing today; He's an on-time God."*

It takes faith to trust God for your healing, deliverance, peace, and joy. When you've been hurt many times, sometimes you lose faith in being healed of the situation. Therefore, another mask is added.

I went from hurt to more hurt in that marriage. One day I told God that I wanted to be saved even if no one else in my house wanted to be saved. It wasn't that I wasn't saved, but I had to let God know that salvation was my choice and it was not just because I wanted him to deliver me from the hurt, I was experiencing.

I removed one mask, but in the process - I gained two more. Doubt and worry took its' place. I totally surrendered to God. I let him know that I wanted and needed him. I confessed and the wicked one heard it as well. The enemy used my husband, my children and my own body against me.

And it happened again - another mask! More hurt and pain.

Ex-husband; children - I forgive you.

I found out that falling in love with Jesus was the best thing I had ever done. My love for Jesus and my new lease on life helped get me back on my feet and caused many masks to be removed.

To get rid of the masks - fear, doubt, and worry, you have to get into God and the Word – Jesus, Who is the Word. Not just for a day or two, a month or a year, or even just when things are not going right but for the rest of your life. Even then, there will still be hurt but God will help you deal with it. God's Word states in Psalm 34:19 (KJV) that the righteous will have many afflictions, but don't worry, the Lord will deliver you out of them all. Not some but ALL! So - remove the fear, doubt and worry from your heart.

Now, after learning the Word and trying to remove the different mask I wore, I decided to go back to school and get my last degree. After I started my degree program, I began to worry about school and fear took a seat in my heart. It was fear of the unknown. Fear and worry are bad spirits. When they are attached to you, only God, through fasting and prayer can free you from them.

Yet again, another mask was added. I knew what the bible said about worry, but I was in a place that I had never been before in my mind. I was overwhelmed to the point that I was not able to let the Word work and I started doing really bad in school. I was dealing with the stress of school, an unfaithful husband, two of my children were locked up and my body was failing me.

I was in a total state of unrest!

But God!

God assured me that if He was for me, He was more than the whole world against me.

Unfortunately, another mask found its' way into my life.

As if I had not lost enough family members, from 2003 to 2010, I lost three sisters, one brother and my grandmother who was my mother since I was three. I had to put on a big mask of bravery to be able to hold the family together. In 2013, it started all over again. From 2013 to 2017, I lost three brothers, two sisters, two brother in-laws, a sister-in-law, a niece and my mother.

The masks continued! As soon as I took off one - two or three more came! I was worried about how I was going to pay for these funerals. I had already paid for or contributed to past family members funerals. It was as if I was the one who was designated to do this! Worry became a big issue for me!

Because there was so much going on - school, multiple deaths, and the stress that came with them; by this time, I was just so tired of the different problems. I cried out to the Lord! I prayed for the Lord to help me to remove these masks. I prayed and I knew that God heard me. Slowly, things began to get better.

Scriptures to Read Concerning Fear, Doubt & Worry

Fear
II Timothy 1:7
For God hath not given us the spirit of fear; but of power, and of love, and of a sound mind.

Isaiah 41:10
Fear thou not; for I am with thee: be not dismayed; for I am thy God: I will strengthen thee; yea, I will help thee; yea, I will uphold thee with the right hand of my righteousness.

Joshua 1:9
Have not I commanded thee? Be strong and of a good courage; be not afraid, neither be thou dismayed for the Lord thy God is with thee whithersoever thou goes.

Doubt
Genesis 17:16-17
And I will bless her (Sarah), and give thee a son also of her: yea, I will bless her, and she shall be a mother of nations; kings of people shall be of her. Then Abraham fell upon his face, and laughed, and said in his heart, Shall a child be born unto him that is an hundred years old? and shall Sarah, that is ninety years old, bear?

St. Matthew 11:4-6
Jesus answered and said unto them, God and shew John again those things which ye do hear and see: The blind receive their

sight, and the lame walk, the lepers are cleansed and the deaf hear, the dead are raised up and the poor have the gospel preached to them.

St. John 20:25
The other disciples therefore said unto him, we have seen the Lord. But he said unto them, Except I shall see in his hands the print of the nails and put my finger into the print of the nails, and thrust my hand into his side, I will not believe.

James 1: 8
A double minded man is unstable in all his ways.

Worry

Philippians 4:6-7
Be careful for nothing; but in everything by prayer and supplication with thanksgiving let your request be made known unto God. And the peace of God which passeth all understanding, shall keep your hearts and mind through Christ Jesus.

I Peter 5:7
Casting all your cares upon him; for he careth for you.

St. Matthew 6:25
Therefore I say unto you, Take no thought for your life, what ye shall eat, or what ye shall drink; nor yet for body, what ye shall put on. Is not the life more than meat, and the body than raiment?

CHAPTER THREE
Loneliness

I am reminded of a time when I had so many things going wrong in my life. Well, another time. I called on the Lord and He told me that He would work it out for me. During that time, I experienced loneliness along with pain and hurt. That threesome was a bad combination to try to mask. When loneliness was not eating me up, I had pain and hurt trying to tear me down.

God began to remind me that He is faithful. When God tells you something you can count on it; He will bring it to pass. Isaiah 55:10-11(KJV) gives us a good illustration of that when it tells us "That as the rain cometh down and the snow from heaven and water the earth, that it may bring forth and bud, so shall my word be that goeth forth out of my mouth, it shall not return unto me void, but it shall accomplish that which I please and it shall prosper in the thing whereto I sent it."

As I sought the Lord, He began to help me remove the different masks. He began to take away the hurt, fear, worry, and doubt, but the loneliness was masked behind so many unfinished things.

Since hurt is a tool the enemy uses, I guess you are

wondering why I keep bringing it up. It is because hurt is, as I just stated, a big tool the enemy uses to keep you bound, locked up and lonely. If we don't give our lives to the Lord, we will be consumed by hurt and loneliness and overwhelmed with the different masks.

After years of hiding my feelings and parading around with multiple masks like nothing was wrong, I sought the Lord concerning my loneliness. He helped me to remove that mask. I also wore masks of sickness, struggle, sadness, loneliness, regret, disappointment, rejection, not feeling good enough, and many other masks. One day God spoke to my heart and told me that He was working things out for me. He would speak to my heart when I got to a point that I felt like giving up. He reminded me that He is God, He is still on the throne and He would work things out for my good. That reminded me of the scripture - Romans 8:28 (KJV) "And we know that all things work together for good to those who love God, to those who are the called according to His purpose."

Loneliness is a spirit and if you are not careful, it will creep up on you even in a house full of people. It will ride your heart, mind and back, whispering in your ear, telling you that no one loves you and no one is concerned about you. Some of these spirits you cannot get rid of except by fasting and praying.

God said in His Word that the temptations - whether loneliness, doubt, hurt, fear, worry or unforgiveness - He has the key to getting rid of them. The key is keeping our mind stayed on Jesus. When I heard my grandmother and others say that, I thought - how can you keep your mind on Jesus all day and night? I came to understand that praying, having a song of God in your heart, reading your Word, and talking about Jesus, who is the Word, will keep Him on your mind.

Keep prayer in your heart.

Make sure you repent.

Focus your mind on God so nothing can enter your mind to contaminate your thoughts.

Whatever you do, don't re-open the door to loneliness, fear, doubt, worry, or unforgiveness. Those spirits will tear you down faster than a dog chewing on a bone.

Give your life to God and let Jesus become your Savior. You don't have to be lonely. Invite the Holy Ghost to abide in your spirit and He will ward off those evil spirits in Jesus name.

Scriptures to Read Concerning Loneliness

Psalm 27:10

When my father and my mother forsake me, then the Lord will
take me up.

I Samuel 12:22

For the Lord will not forsake his people for his great name' sake:
because it hath pleased the Lord to make you his people.

Psalm 25:16

Turn thee unto me and have mercy upon me; for I am desolate and
afflicted.

Isaiah 41:10

Fear thou not; for I am with thee: be not dismayed; for I am thy
God: I will uphold thee with the right hand of my righteousness.

I Peter 5:7

Casting all you care upon him; for he careth for you.

I Corinthian 10:13

There is no temptation taken you, but such as is common to man:
but God is faithful; who will not suffer you to be tempted above
that ye are able; but will with the temptation also make a way to
escape that ye may be able to bear it.

CHAPTER FOUR
Unforgiveness / Forgiveness

I have encountered all the spirits that I wrote about. They are bad, but I believe unforgiveness is the worst of them all. I thank God that He did not allow that spirit to grip me too tight. Yes, there was a time when I carried a spirit of unforgiveness. Unforgiveness is bad because it will not allow you to rest. It keeps you up at night thinking that someone is doing you wrong or mistreating you. That spirit will, as the kids say, "mess your head up" and keep you in constant panic mode.

Do you remember the movie *"Sleeping With the Enemy?"* Well, just think, you know that you are not being treated right but God will use you as a Hosea. He will tell you to go to this person and ask for forgiveness. That is what He did to me. When I went to them and asked them to forgive me of anything I had done to them, they replied that I hadn't done anything to them. They admitted that they were the one who was in the wrong. At that moment God freed me! He spoke to my heart and said that is what He wanted me to see.

Jesus love is so great toward us. When we ask for forgiveness, the Bible says, "He will turn again, he will have compassion upon us; he will subdue our iniquities and thou will cast all their sins into the depths of the sea." Micah 7:19 (KJV). He requires us to do likewise. I did not say it would be easy when someone has done all manner of evil against you, but we have to remember - what would Jesus do?

The Bible definition for unforgiveness is: a grudge against someone who has offended you.

Another definition of unforgiveness from the Google dictionary is: unwilling or unable to forgive; having or making no allowance for error or weakness; an unforgiving environment where false moves can prove fatal - holding a grudge against someone who has offended you.

Jesus talked about forgiveness and the Bible's answer for forgiveness is the act of pardoning an offender. In the Bible, the Greek word for "forgiveness" translated literally means "to let go," as when a person does not demand payment for a debt. Jesus used this comparison when he taught His followers to pray: "forgive us our sins, for we ourselves also forgive everyone who is in debt to us." Luke 11:14 (KJV)

Likewise, in his parable of the unmerciful slave, Jesus equated forgiveness with canceling a debt. Matthew 18:23-25 (KJV)

We forgive others when we let go of resentment and give

up any claim to be compensated for the hurt or loss we have suffered. The Bible teaches that unselfish love is the basis for true forgiveness, "since love does not keep account of the injury." I Corinthians 13:4-5 (KJV)

I had to seek God for help. He helped me to pull off the mask of unforgiveness as well. When I pulled that one off - relief came to my mind and soul. The song my former first lady used to sing came to mind - "Oh the joy that came to me when I realized that I was free, when Jesus found me and wrapped His loving arms around me, Oh the joy that came to me."

I love the Lord! He has been so good to me. He has helped me to see so much about myself. He has shown me that I am important. I am beautiful. I don't have to fear, worry, be in doubt or have unforgiveness in my heart because He came to set me free. He said in His word - "if the Son therefore shall make you free, ye shall be free indeed." St John 8:36 (KJV)

Scriptures to Read Concerning Forgiveness

Colossian 3:13

Forbearing one another, and forgiving one another, if any man have a quarrel against any, even as Christ forgave you, so also do ye.

St. Matthew 6:14

For if ye forgive men their trespasses, your heavenly Father will also forgive you.

St. Luke 17:3

Take head to yourselves: if thy brother trespass against thee, rebuke him; and if he repent, forgive him.

I John 1:9

If we confess our sins, he is faithful and just to forgive us our sins, and to cleanse us from all unrighteousness.

Isaiah 43:25

I, even I, am he that blotteth out thy transgressions for mine own sake and will not remember thy sins.

Ephesians 1:7

In whom we have redemption through his blood, the forgiveness of sins, according to the riches of his grace.

CHAPTER FIVE
Freedom In Jesus

"If the Son therefore shall make you free, ye shall be free indeed." St. John 8:36 (KJV)

I am free. Free from worry. Free from stress. Free from fear, doubt, and loneliness. Yes, the enemy tries to bring them back. They try to rear their ugly head when I am not prayed up, or when I'm feeling low. But when I call on Jesus, all things change! The fear, doubt, unbelief, and unforgiveness has to flee.

The masks are coming off and Barbara – (*insert your name here)* - is coming out. I want to let the world know that I am free. Freedom is an action; a state of mind and being. Today and forever more, I choose to be free.

I cannot tell you how your freedom will come, but I can tell you who it will come through. That is Jesus, and only Jesus. When you surrender your life totally to Him, He will fight for you and make everything work out for your good. It may not be the way you want it to be, but it will be for your good.

Freedom! I am free. Freedom. I am free, I am free! There is a song which goes something like this "Oh the joy that came to me, when I realize I was finally free, when He found me, (because I was truly and hopelessly lost), wrapped His arms around me, oh the joy that came to me. I am free!

The enemy did not want me to write this book because he knew that it would help many of God's people. Today, I tell you - you do not have to wear those masks anymore. You may not have on the ones that I wore, but whatever your masks are - you don't have to wear them anymore. As the song says, "when you call on Jesus all things are possible." Jesus also spoke these same words in the Bible.

Let us be free by calling on the name of Jesus.

Scriptures To Read Concerning Freedom

Galatian 5:1
Stand fast therefore in the liberty wherewith Christ hath made us free, and be not entangled again with the yoke of bondage.

St. John 8:36
If the Son therefore shall make you free, ye shall be free indeed.

II Corinthian 3:17
Now the Lord is that Spirit: and where the Spirit of the Lord is, there is liberty.

Psalm 34:19
Many are the afflictions of the righteous: but the Lord delivereth him out of them all.

Psalm 119:45
And I will walk at liberty; for I seek thy precepts.

ABOUT THE AUTHOR

Barbara A. Taylor was born in a small town in Joiner, Arkansas to the Late Osie Lee and Bernice Dawkins. She is the first of 22 of her mother's children. She is the mother of five children, grandmother of eight, and great grandmother of two. She is honest; a woman of integrity, faith and a praying woman of God. Currently, she is working on a Ph.D. in Education and Organizational Leadership.

God has taken her through many things and now she is sharing some of the knowledge with others to help them through the perils of life. This woman of God has gone through the water and the fire. Now, she is back to help others through sickness, pain, sorrowfulness, hurt, lost, fear, and sadness. Her desire is to help them get to a state of freedom as well.

About 22 years ago, God gave her an email ministry. Now, she shares scriptures online via Facebook. If you want to be encouraged every morning, just look up Barbara A. Taylor #GoldNuggets!

Made in the USA
Columbia, SC
30 January 2023

11238217R00020